REVISED and ENLARGED EDITION

BASEBALL

By Dick Siebert
Baseball Coach, University of Minnesota

and Otto Vogel
Former Baseball Coach, University of Iowa

ATHLETIC
INSTITUTE
SERIES

STERLING PUBLISHING CO., INC.

NEW YORK

ATHLETIC INSTITUTE SERIES

Baseball
Basketball
Girls' Basketball
Girls' Gymnastics

Gymnastics
Judo
Table Tennis
Tumbling and Trampolining

Wrestling

Eighth Printing, 1975
Copyright © 1968, 1965
by The Athletic Institute
Published by Sterling Publishing Co., Inc.
419 Park Avenue South, New York, N.Y. 10016
Manufactured in the United States of America
All rights reserved
Library of Congress Catalog Card No.: 68-18803
Sterling ISBN 0–8069–4300–9 Trade
4301–7 Library

Table of Contents

1922545

Cricket

1. History

In old colonial days the aristocracy of young New York spent leisure hours playing or watching cricket, a game brought from England by the settlers. At the same time the people of Boston were playing a somewhat similar game called "rounders." These two imported games, cricket and rounders, were the joint ancestors of the great American game of baseball.

Rounders

*Making
their own
equipment*

The feeder

Colonial youngsters actually started the development. When they wanted to play baseball they had to make their own equipment out of whatever materials they could find. With the same originality, they made up their own rules. They started with the rules of rounders. One player, the "feeder," would toss the ball to the "striker," underhand and slowly, to be sure the striker hit it. The striker would hit it as far as he could

The striker

The playing field

The scout

and then try to run to a nearby stump or stake and back before either the feeder or the "scout" could retrieve the ball and throw it with all his force to hit the runner before he could reach "home." This was the rowdy, simple game that eventually became baseball.

Hitting the runner

9

Town Ball

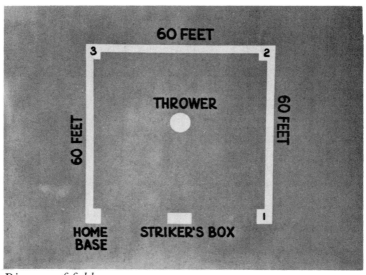

Diagram of field

The New York Game

As more people joined the game, they simply set out more stakes around which the striker had to run before getting back home. The youngsters called their game "Town Ball." The Town Ball field was developing toward a baseball diamond as we know it today.

Meanwhile, back in New York, former cricket enthusiasts were developing their game in a similar direction, replacing the wickets with four bases. They called their game "The New York Game." Their field began to look like a modern baseball diamond.

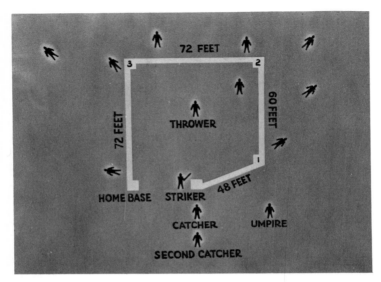

Diagram of New York Game

Alexander Cartwright designing the diamond

12

The first baseball game

In 1845, a young surveyor named Alexander Cartwright gave the orderly touch of a draftsman to developing the game. He designed the first baseball diamond. On a field in Hoboken, New Jersey, in 1846, the new game was tried in a match between the New York Nine and the Knickerbocker Club. By the new rules there were nine men on a team. A turn at bat was called a "hand" and a circuit of the bases was called an "ace." The first team to score twenty-one aces won the game.

The solid ball

The broad bat

Feeding the ball to the striker

Soldiers ready to play

The ball was made of hard, solid rubber. It was as lively as a tennis ball but as hard on the hands as a present-day baseball. The bat had a broad, flat hitting side. It wasn't difficult to hit the ball with a bat as broad as that, particularly since the thrower didn't really pitch. His job was to feed the ball to the striker, making it easy for the striker to hit it.

The game increased steadily in popularity. When the Civil War brought together men from all the States, many north-eastern soldiers carried the equipment of the New York Game with them. They played whenever they could. Westerners learned the game from easterners, and southern prisoners in

Playing in a prison camp

The town welcomes the players

northern camps were fascinated as they watched. The game's appeal cut through sectional differences, finding response in the basic Americanism of both armies. It was a sport that struck a key chord in the spirit of the new country.

Returning veterans took the game home with them. Soon each hamlet in every state had its ball team. Teams visited for matches, and a match was the occasion for a local holiday and all-day celebration. The players were the heroes of the hour —if they won. Americans were taking baseball to their hearts.

A contest between hamlets

Outwitting the batter

Batting becomes harder with a round bat

A bruised catcher

The rules, equipment and playing technique were steadily improving to make the game one of skill and stamina. The easy cricket style was disappearing. The pitcher began to pitch with all his speed and cunning. Now his object was to prevent the batter from hitting, if possible. The batter used a round bat now, finding it considerably harder to handle than the flat cricket bat.

Part of the gallantry of the game was when the noble catcher lasted nine innings without glove or mask, having to catch the ball on the first bounce. The ninth inning often found him battered but unbowed. Amid the jeers of the he-man

*Caught
with his
gloves on*

*A sensible
catcher*

players, catchers then started to wear tight flesh-colored gloves, hoping not to be noticed. But they were noticed and finally one courageous catcher faced the crowd wearing not only a padded mitt, but a mask as well. Now he could move up and catch the ball before it bounced. Baseball was becoming a game of skill, and they couldn't be skilled with bloody noses and raw hands.

Soon the rest of the team adopted protective equipment and since then baseball has developed steadily in speed, skill and precision. Today baseball has taken a grip on the imagination of Americans everywhere. It has become a national institution, America's most representative game.

Protection for the whole team

Photo 1

Today's regulation baseball is very different from the hard rubber sphere of the New York Game. Now it has a cork or rubber center with a tight wool winding and a horsehide cover (Photo 1).

Today's bats are scientifically designed and standardized in various sizes to suit the size, strength and hitting style of the player.

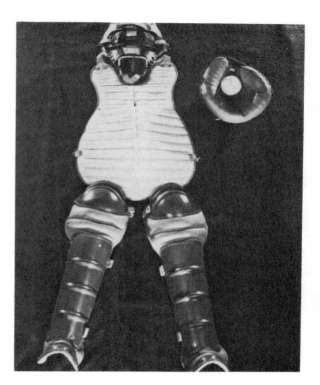

Photo 2

Every player, regardless of his playing position, now wears a mitt or a glove.

Although the rules of the game prescribe certain weights and sizes for this equipment, there is a wide variety of styles, each style having been carefully designed and manufactured to increase the players' skill. Photo 2 shows how the once bloody but unbowed catcher is now protected fully by a mask, a chest protector and shin guards. Since he is a key member of the team, his equipment is designed to allow freedom of action as well as to provide protection.

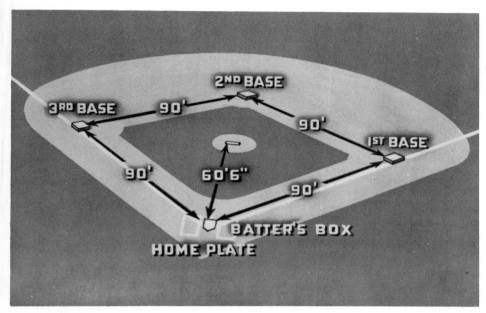

Diagram of field

Home plate and the batters' boxes

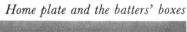

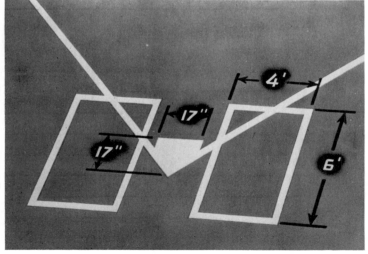

Strange as it may seem, today's playing field is not greatly different from Alexander Cartwright's original design. Still diamond shaped, it has remained 90 feet on all sides. Lines extending straight out from home plate beyond first and third base separate fair from foul territory. The batter's box on either side of home plate is 4 feet by 6 feet. Home plate itself is 17 inches wide and 17 inches from the front to the back corner.

The pitcher and catcher, as a pair, are "the battery." The distance from the front of the pitcher's plate to the back corner of home plate is 60 feet, 6 inches. The first baseman, second baseman, shortstop and third baseman are the infielders. Completing the nine-man team are the outfielders, the right fielder, center fielder and left fielder.

Diagram of the players

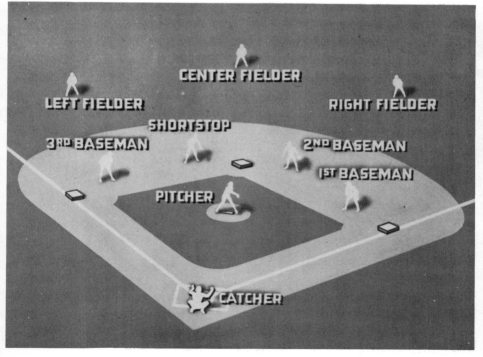

A modern game

Photo 3

Timing of the hit

The tempo of modern baseball has been greatly heightened since the days of Town Ball and the New York Game. The pitcher must now pitch the ball with all his speed and skill to try to prevent the batter from hitting it. The strike zone is the width of home plate between the batter's shoulders and his kneecaps when he is standing in a normal crouch (Photo 3).

With the pitched ball traveling as fast as 90 miles an hour, the batter has less than half a second to decide whether or not to swing at it. After he has decided, he still has to use part of the half second to get the bat around to meet the ball in exactly the right place. Actually the ball is within the reach

When the ball is within range of hitting

Hit and go

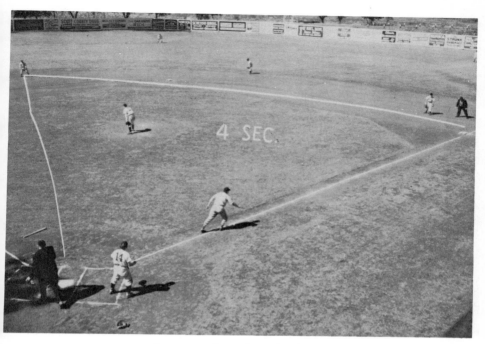

A runner tries to beat the throw

of his bat for only 1/50th of a second. This is why hitting takes a keen eye, good judgment, a fine sense of timing and well controlled strength.

After hitting the ball, the batter must run to first base as fast as he can. A good runner can make it in less than 4 seconds. In that short time, the whole defensive strategy of the opposing team goes into action. While the batter runs 90 feet, the defensive team must get the ball over to first base. Four seconds— one—two—three—four—is all it takes for a play in baseball.

A quick throw to first

Most of the time the fielder can't even take time to straighten up to throw. Without wasting a fraction of a second he must get it to first base. His throw should be so accurate that the first baseman doesn't have to take his foot off the base to catch the ball. In close decisions at first base, those split seconds make all the difference between defeat and victory.

When a runner tries to steal second, it's the catcher who has some split-second work to do. The runner starts with the pitch (Photo 4). Now the catcher has less than three seconds to catch

The runner is safe

Photo 4

Photo 5

Photo 6

Planning the game

the ball and to throw it down to second base ahead of the
runner (Photo 5). Over that distance, about 130 feet, his throw
has to be so accurate that the second baseman can catch it
right down near the base to save those precious parts of a
second lost in bringing down a higher throw (Photo 6). Through
all the excitement of a game the catcher must keep his com-
posure and be the calm strategist of the game. He signals every
pitch, watches every play position and plans the defensive
strategy, play by play.

Developing skills through practice

When all of these factors are realized, it's easy to understand that modern baseball is a game of finely developed skill, accurate judgment, speed of both mind and body and strength of well disciplined muscles. In a young player, all of these abilities can be developed through two basic steps. The first is a sure knowledge of the fundamentals of individual skills, and the second is steady, consistent practice that stresses the fundamentals of the game.

Movement of your body adds the maximum power to your throw.

2. Throwing

If any single skill in baseball is more important than all others, that skill is throwing. Unless every man on the team can throw accurately and with speed enough to beat a runner from whatever position he plays, the team cannot be strong on defense.

Photo 1

There are three types of throws. The underhand throw (Photo 1) is used when it's important to get the ball away fast and there isn't time to straighten up.

Photo 2

Photo 3

Photo 4

The sidearm throw (Photo 2) is good for short, quick throws, but it should be used only in emergencies by most ball players. By far the most used and most valuable throw is the overhand throw (Photos 3 and 4). It is more accurate and has more power and control than any other throw. If you are a beginning ball player, learn the overhand throw first, practicing it until all the fundamentals are natural, and you have achieved speed and control. Then the other two throws will develop naturally.

Photo 5

Your grip on the ball is the most important factor in control, so adopt the correct grip at the start and use the same grip on every throw. Even in practice, never vary your grip. The feel of the ball is so important that you should never practice with anything but a regulation baseball. The correct grip is shown in Photos 5 and 6—the ball held between your thumb and first two fingers, with your third finger resting lightly against the ball. Two fingers are slightly spread on top and your thumb is on the bottom, directly below the fingers.

Photo 6 indicates what the correct grip looks like from your own view. Your first two fingers grip across the seam, because this gives you better control and helps you put spin on the ball.

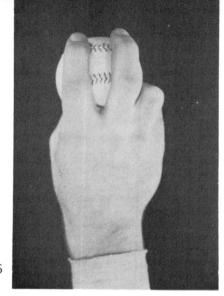

Photo 6

As the ball leaves your hand on the throw, it rolls off of your fingertips, giving the ball a spinning motion (Photo 7). Learn to give it the same spin on every throw—otherwise control is difficult.

Photo 7

Step 1

As your arm comes forward in the throw, your upper arm and forearm are at an approximate right angle, your upper arm about parallel with the ground (Step 1).

Step 2

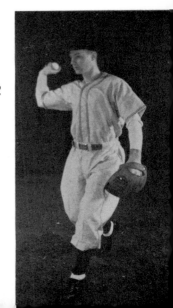

The crucial point of your throw is just as the ball is about to leave your hand (Step 2). Here your wrist is playing the important part because the final action before releasing the ball is

a snap of the wrist that gives your throw its last ounce of power (Step 3). This snap action is an essential part of every throw and it can make or break you as a defensive ball player.

Step 1

Practice the snap alone for a while. Stand in the release position with your body upright, upper arm straight out from the shoulder, and your forearm vertical. Lay your wrist back as far as it will go without taking your forearm back with it (Step 1). Now throw the ball without moving any part of your body except your wrist and hand.

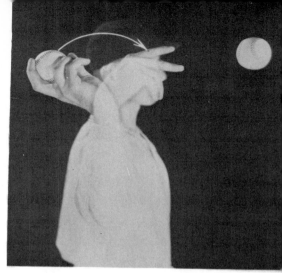

Step 2

Snap your hand forward from the wrist with all the power you can put into it, and throw the ball as far and straight as you can (Step 2). Practice this snap for a while and you'll feel your wrist settling down into an easy, rhythmic throw.

Add more power by putting arm action into the throw. Keep your body erect and lay your whole arm back as far as it will go, keeping your upper arm approximately parallel with the ground (Step 3). Stretch your arm back until you can feel the

Step 3

Step 4

pull across your chest. Your forearm is laid back from the elbow and your hand laid back on the wrist as far as both will go (Step 4).

The movement starts in your shoulder as you bring your arm forward like a whip. Your elbow leads the movement of the arm (Step 5). As your upper arm comes forward, your forearm stays back and your wrist still farther back. When the forward movement of your elbow is even with your shoulder,

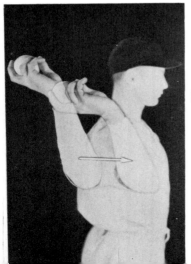

Step 5

Step 6

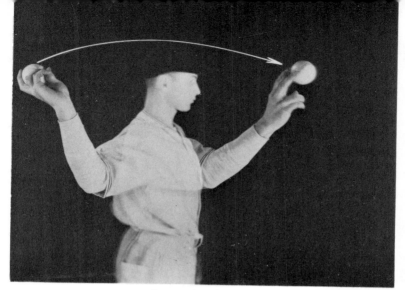

Arm and wrist action

the whip action continues through your forearm, wrist and hand, snapping the ball forward from the release position (Step 6). Then the whole arm follows through. Practice this movement for a while, as it is the crucial part of your throw. Throw the ball as far and straight as you can. Remember the whip action—let your fingers feel like the snapping end of a whip. Remember that the elbow leads the movement, building up force until the snap of the wrist.

When a fielder gets the ball and starts to throw, his first object is to get his whole body and arm laid back in order to whip the ball forward. From the position shown in Step 1 the

Step 1

weight shifts immediately to the back foot as the throwing arm swings backward toward the full layback position (Step 2). At the same time the body is swinging back until, in the full layback position, your weight is fully on your rear foot and your body and throwing arm are stretched backward, reaching back to get as much power as possible into the forward throw (Step 3). Simultaneous with the backward movement of the

Step 3

Step 4

Step 5

throwing arm and body, your front foot starts forward toward the target.

Remember that from the fielding position, your throwing arm and body are stretched backward like an extended whip, ready to snap forward in the throw (Step 4). After a momentary pause in the layback position, your forward foot completes its stride and your body starts moving forward. As your weight comes onto your front foot, your front leg braces to act as a firm support for the throw as it points toward the target (Step 5).

Step 6

As your forward leg braces, your hips thrust forward and pivot around square with the target, your whole body moving forward against your braced front leg (Step 6). As your body comes forward, the whiplike movement goes on through your shoulder into your arm, and ends in a snap of the wrist as you release the ball (Step 7). The arm movement is exactly as you practiced it earlier. All the power of your body, from your feet

Step 7

Step 8

through your legs, hips, back, shoulders and arm to your wrist, has been built up and is all released as you let the ball go. But your movement does not stop here. Your whole body follows through. Throw your hand forward after the ball (Step 8). Your arm keeps on moving in a full follow-through. Let your body swing around naturally on your forward foot as your back leg swings around into a balanced position (Step 9).

Step 9

This is the basic throw of baseball—a whiplike movement from a full layback to a full, free follow-through after the ball. These basic fundamentals apply to all throws.

Photo 1

Infielders do not often have time for a full overhand throw. They get the ball away faster with a snap overhand throw. From the fielding position they get into throwing position as fast as possible, bringing their throwing arm up to the layback position the shortest and fastest way (Photo 1). From this point the throw is very similar to the full overhand throw.

Photo 2

The throwing movement is the same sequence of forward movements—the stride toward the target, the whipping movement that ends in the wrist to snap the ball forward, and then a normal follow-through (Photo 2).

The sidearm throw is another throw an infielder may use in special situations (Photo 3). The only difference between the full sidearm and the overhand throw is that in the full sidearm

Photo 3

Photo 4

the arm is held out to the side with less bend in the elbow throughout the swing and the body pivots more (Photo 4). The whiplike movement that ends with a snap of the wrist as the ball is released and the follow-through is the same as in all other throws.

For shorter, quicker throws the sidearm snap throw may be used. The sidearm snap follows all the fundamental movements of the snap overhand. From a fielding position (Photo 5), bring the ball back to the layback position the shortest, fastest way. Then snap the ball forward as shown in Photo 6.

Photo 5

Photo 6

Photo 7

On certain plays the underhand snap throw can be used. The movement is shown in Photo 7. It contains the same fundamentals of all other throws, but the body does not straighten up.

Throwing is one of the most important basic skills of baseball, and skill at throwing is every man's obligation to the team. But as throwing is not necessarily a natural ability, a good throwing arm can only be acquired by consistent practice and careful observance of these fundamentals.

Dropping down for a grounder

3. Fielding

Fielding is a responsibility of every man on the team, no matter what position he plays. Every player of a winning team must be able to field both ground balls and fly balls. Like all the other positions and skills of baseball, skill at fielding is a combination of natural ability and constant practice in the fundamentals of the fielding movements.

In the basic fielding position while you are learning to field ground balls, keep close to the ground, so close that your hands touch the ground when hanging naturally. It's easier to come up after a ball than drop down for it, so *keep low for ground balls*.

Step 1

When ready to field a ball, your heels are close together, weight on the balls of your feet, knees turned outward, body bent slightly forward, eyes on the ball. The palms are turned outward, little fingers together, fingers downward (Step 1). To get the feel of fielding, take this position and have someone roll a ball to you.

Let the ball roll into your glove and, as it does, your throwing hand rolls over and traps it in the glove (Step 2). After you have learned to field a ground ball in this manner, you are ready to advance to the fielding position that is usually used in the game.

Step 2

Step 1

Step 2

Step 1 is the waiting position before the pitch. Face the batter as you watch the ball, with your feet comfortably spread, knees slightly bent, and weight slightly forward. As the ball is pitched, shift your weight slightly forward so that you will be able to get a fast start in any direction (Step 2). If the ball is hit in your direction, you'll have to get in front of it as fast as you can.

When the ball is hit fairly hard and directly at you, come in on the ball if you have time (Step 3). Play the ball. Don't let it

Step 3

Step 4

play you. As the ball nears you, set yourself in fielding position—
feet comfortably spread, right foot slightly behind the left, body
low with knees well bent, back fairly straight and eyes "glued"
on the ball (Step 4). Assume this position after you have learned
to field the ball properly in the basic fielding position. Keep
your eyes on the ball as it settles into the glove, and then bring
your throwing hand over it to trap it securely (Step 5).

Step 5

Photo 1

Most ground balls will be fielded below the belt, which means that the fingers will be pointing downward, palms facing the ball and your little fingers close together (Photo 1). Sometimes a ball will hop high and above the belt. In this case your fingers will be pointing upward, palms once more facing the ball and your thumbs close together, as shown in Photo 2.

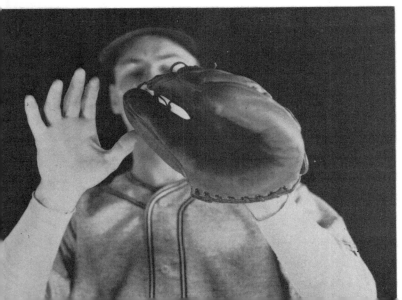

Photo 2

Photo 3

Photo 4

Photos 3 and 4 show the two basic positions for fielding high and low ground balls. Practice these fundamental fielding positions by having someone hit balls straight to you.

On slow ground balls hit directly at you, come in fast and keep your body low. Then place the glove on the ground well in front of you, allow the ball to roll into it and clasp it immediately with your throwing hand (Photo 5). If the play must be made in a hurry, you might have to pick up the ball

Photo 5

Photo 6

with your bare hand. In this case, field the ball in front of your right foot, with your body to the left of the ball (Photo 6). Do not attempt this, however, until you have become an adept fielder.

Of course, many ground balls are hit to the left or the right of the fielder. When fielding a ground ball to either side, turn in the direction of the ball immediately and get in front of it as

A hit to the left or right of a fielder

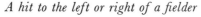

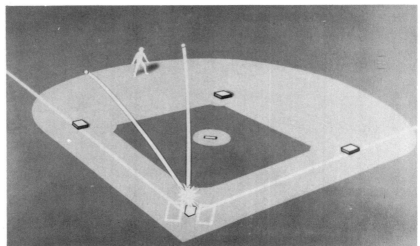

Step 1   Step 2

fast as possible. Keep your body low. Step 1 shows the fielder going for a ground ball to his right. During your run keep your eye on the ball. Never let it out of your focus until you have it in your glove, even if you must field the ball in the position shown in Step 2.

The direction of your run will depend on how hard the ball has been hit. If a hard-hit ball goes to your right, cut straight

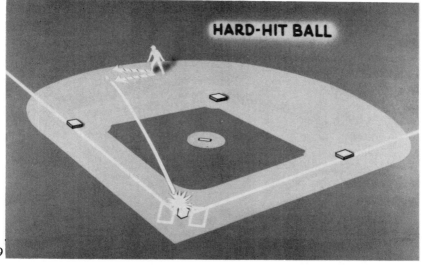

HARD-HIT BALL

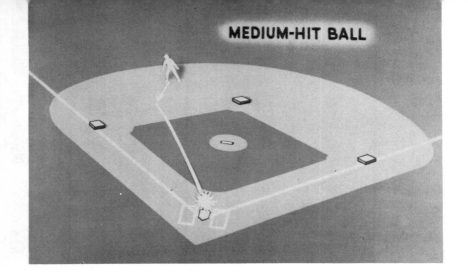

MEDIUM-HIT BALL

across or diagonally back to meet it. For a medium-hit ground ball to the right, run diagonally forward toward the ball. For a slow-hit ball to your right, come in fast and straighter toward the ball. The important thing in direction is to judge the speed of the ball and get in front of it as soon as possible.

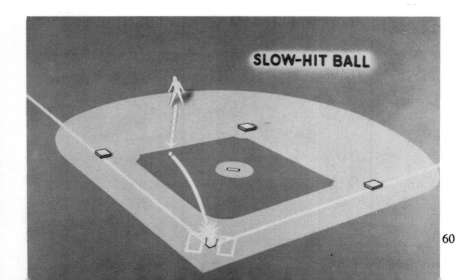

SLOW-HIT BALL

Step 1

Most throws by infielders are to their left. If you're running for a ground ball to your right (Step 1) you'll have to stop and get set for a throw in the opposite direction. In this case stop squarely in front of the ball by jamming your right foot against the ground. Field the ball with your legs apart, your right leg braced. Now your braced leg gives a firm support for your throw back to your left (Step 2). If you have to run to the left

Step 2

Step 1

for a ground ball (Step 1) and do not have time to get in front
of it and get set for the throw, then after fielding the ball on
the run check your momentum as quickly as possible, making
the throw off the right foot and stepping in the direction of the
throw with your left. Step 2 shows how the fielder fields the
ball with his left foot forward. He steps on his right foot to
check his run. He then pivots on his right foot and steps
toward first base with his left foot for the throw.

Step 2

An important point to remember when you get the ball in your glove, don't rush the throw unnecessarily. Set yourself for an overhand throw, then give it everything you have (Step 3).

Step 3

On all fly balls there is one cardinal rule for fielders—get under it fast and wait.

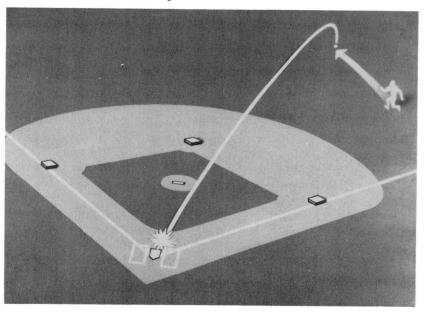

A hit to your right

Step 1

For a fly ball hit either to your right or left, turn in that direction quickly with whatever footwork proves fastest for you. For a fly ball hit straight over your head there is another factor, wind direction, that determines which way you should turn. No fielder should start an inning without first checking the direction of the wind.

For a fly ball hit straight over your head, turn in the direction the wind is blowing. If the wind is blowing from your left, the ball will drift toward your right. Make your first step diagonally backward with your right foot so that you will be moving in the direction of the drift (Step 1).

Try to determine approximately where the ball will fall. Then turn and run to that spot. Never run backward if you

Step 2

can avoid it. Turn around and run after the ball, glancing over your shoulder as you run (Step 2). Get under the ball as soon as you can, get set and wait for it (Step 3).

Step 3

Step 4

Step 5

Step 6

Don't reach for the ball until you are under it. There are two
positions for your hands while catching fly balls. You can hold
your hands with your little fingers together (Step 4); or with
your thumbs together (Step 5). Through practice you will be
able to make an instinctive decision about the position of your
hands on every fly ball. Let the ball drop into your gloved
hand and immediately trap it with the other (Step 6). Then
get the ball into the infield as fast as you can.

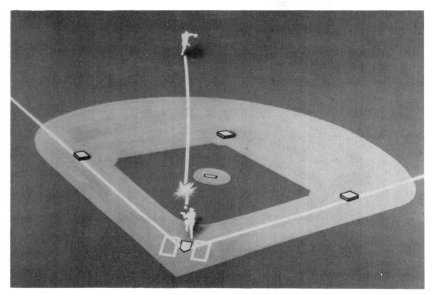

Diagram of the throw

If you are making an exceptionally long throw, such as to home plate, throw the ball at the ground about 30 feet in front of its target and let it hop the rest of the way. This will eliminate overthrows and, in case of a throw to home plate, the ball can be handled for a cut-off if necessary.

What you have learned so far are the basic fundamentals of fielding. If you learn these fundamentals and practice them until all the correct movements are instinctive with you, you will be capable of the alert, skilled fielding that wins ball games.

Successful hitting skill is a combination of three factors— natural ability, confidence and knowledge of the basic fundamentals.

4. Hitting

In the correct grip your hands may be together or only slightly spread, gripping from opposite sides with fingers and

Select a bat that gives you a feeling of control—heavy enough for a good solid swing, but not so heavy that it swings you instead of you swinging it.

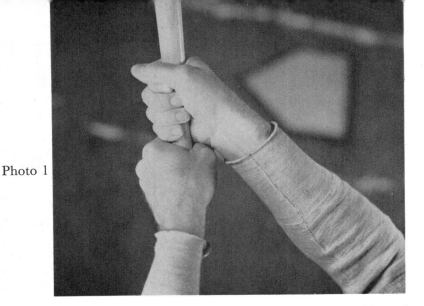

Photo 1

thumbs wrapped well around the handle (Photo 1). Photo 2 shows the alignment of the knuckles of both hands. The second knuckles of your upper hand are lined up somewhere between the base knuckles and the second knuckles of your lower hand.

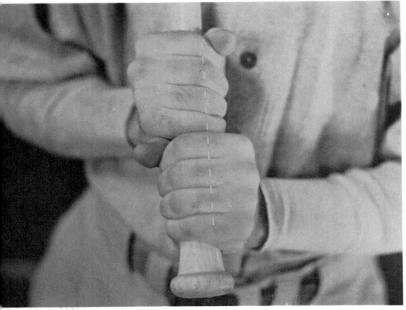

Photo 2

70

Photo 3

There are three types of grip. The end grip (Photo 3) with the hands down close to the knob of the bat, is used by power hitters who want to get the leverage of the full bat length into their swing. The choke grip, with the hands moved well up on the handle, is shown in Photo 4. Hitters who use this grip

Photo 4

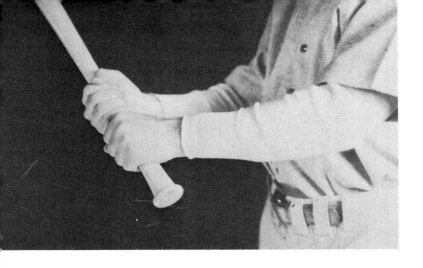

feel that it gives them better control of the bat. The modified
grip (Photo 5) with the lower hand an inch or two from the
knob, is by far the most popular, because hitters feel that it
gives them both control and power. Through most of the swing
the grip is firm but relaxed.

In taking your stance, stand just far enough away from the
plate so that you can grip the bat with either hand and touch

Photo 6

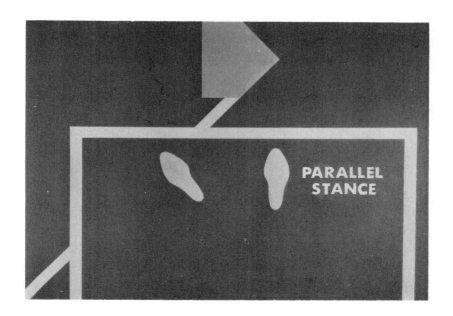

the outside corner of the plate by bending over only slightly (Photo 6). There are three basic types of stance. The parallel stance is with both feet approximately the same distance from the plate. In the closed stance the front foot is closer to the

OPEN STANCE

plate than the rear foot. In the open stance the front foot is farther away from the plate.

If you are a beginning hitter learn the parallel stance first. As you develop your own most comfortable position, you can adapt your stance to a more closed or open stance.

Stand in the correct parallel stance position with your feet

Step 1

Step 2

comfortably spread and your front foot turned slightly toward the pitcher (Step 1). In the ready-to-hit position, as the pitcher is about to deliver the ball, your knees should not be locked but relaxed (Step 2). The important thing is to feel comfortable. Your hips should be square with the plate, parallel with your feet, and relaxed also (Step 3).

Step 3

Step 4

Your arms should be comfortably away from the body and bent at the elbows, as shown in Step 4. Your forward arm guides the swing, its forearm kept almost parallel with the ground.

Step 5

Your back arm puts the power into the swing, so it can drop a little into a comfortable position. Don't drop it too far, and don't pin it against your body. It must be free to move. Your shoulders should be as level as possible, your head firm and steady (Step 5). Keep your eyes on the ball, and be ready to follow it as long as possible from the time the pitcher starts his delivery.

Remember, your ready-to-hit position is firm, steady, comfortable and relaxed. But keep the bat off your shoulder. It should be held well back, at an angle about half way between the vertical and the horizontal. Now you're ready for the swing.

*The
full
swing*

Step 1

Step 2

The hitting swing is actually a powerful coiling and un-coiling of the hips, shoulders and arms around a central axis, the backbone. It is a progressive movement that starts with a pivot of the hips and shoulders, flows through the arms and wrists, and gathers power as it goes, continuing to a full follow-through.

The swing starts as the pitcher delivers the ball. The weight shifts back to the rear foot, and at the same time the front foot reaches forward in a glide to meet the pitch (Step 1). The glide should be natural, neither too long nor too short. Simultaneously the hips, shoulders, arms and bat pivot back around the backbone axis (Step 2). This pivot carries the bat even further back. Now your weight is all on your back foot and your body and arms are tightly coiled around your backbone.

A quick push off the inside of your back foot starts the uncoiling movement. As the forward foot hits the ground, your whole front leg braces. The forward pivot of the hips has just started, and from this point on you swing against your braced front leg (Step 3).

Step 3

The timing of the swing is such that your hands are well in front of your body before the bat is squared around to meet the ball. The weight of your body is all on your forward foot, and your whole left side is firm just before the ball reaches the hitting zone. At this point your wrists come into action (Step 4). As you swing the bat toward the ball, your wrists and hands

Step 4

Step 5

are in the position shown in Step 5. As your bat contacts the ball, your wrists snap and roll over into the position shown in Step 6. Step 7 indicates your wrist action from the snap to the

Step 6

Step 7—Top view

Step 8

Step 9

roll-over. First the snap as your bat contacts the ball. Then the roll-over as you continue around toward your follow-through.

Simultaneously with the wrist snap, your back hip goes into the ball and your forward hip is thrown out of the way (Step 8). The ball has been hit but you continue swinging. As you do, your back foot pivots in on the ball of the foot until your heel lifts off the ground. Your toe stays on the ground to keep your balance. The bat is still swinging (Step 9). Let it swing around naturally in a full, free follow-through (Step 10). Don't try to stop it. Let it stop naturally, and let the weight of your body continue through over the front foot.

The swing is a controlled, powerful movement of all your muscles to swing the bat in a level flat arc. Remember that it is a coiling and uncoiling of your body and arms around your backbone, building up power to be released all together at the exact instant your bat hits the ball. Practice this swing, making sure you follow all the fundamentals, and you can become a high average hitter.

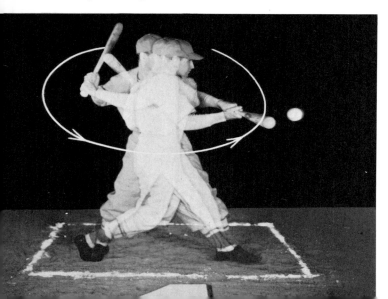

*The
complete
swing*

84

Photo 1

BUNTING

Bunting is an entirely separate phase of hitting, and uses altogether different fundamentals. There are two types of bunts—the sacrifice bunt (Photo 1) and the bunt for a base hit.

The sacrifice bunt is used to advance a runner already on a base and, since the opposition usually expects it, this bunt is made with the whole body square to the pitcher (Photo 2).

Photo 2

Photo 3

Photo 4

Swinging your front foot

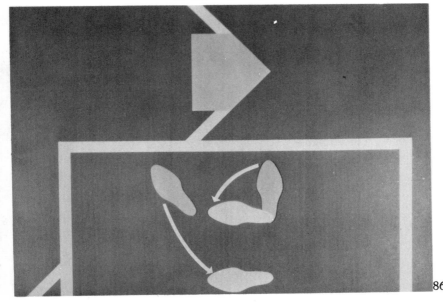

86

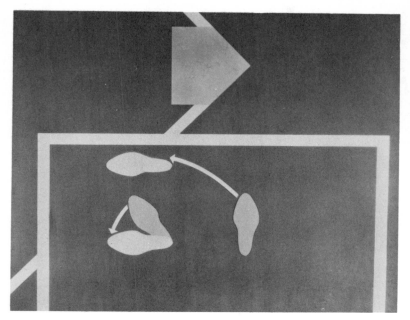

Swinging your back foot

The shift from normal ready-to-hit stance to the sacrifice bunting stance is made just before the pitcher releases the ball (Photos 3 and 4).

There are two methods of making this shift. The first method requires the shift of only one foot. If you stand close to the plate, pivot on your back foot until it points toward the pitcher and swing your front foot back even with it in a comfortable stance. If you stand farther away from the plate, pivot on your front foot and swing your back foot up even with it.

Shifting both feet

The second method of shifting requires the movement of both feet. The front foot moves back away from the plate and the rear foot moves up to a position even with the front foot.

Photos 1 and 2 show a batter using the second method of bunting—for a base hit. From the ready-to-hit position, the front foot has moved into the position shown in Photo 1. Then the rear foot moves up parallel with the front foot, as shown in Photo 2.

Photo 1

Photo 2

Photo 3

Regardless of which method of shifting you use, the fundamentals of bunting are the same. As you pivot, slide your upper
hand up on the bat to a position close to the trade mark. The
lower hand remains steady and firm (Photo 3). The upper
hand grips very lightly, four fingers underneath and thumb on
top. The grip is so light with this hand that the bat just rests
on the fingers (Photo 4). The forearm of the forward arm

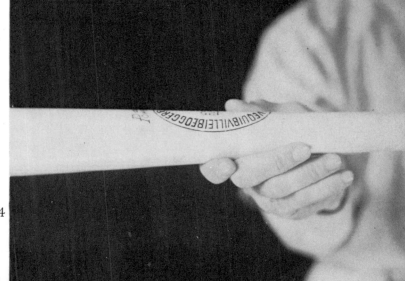

Photo 4

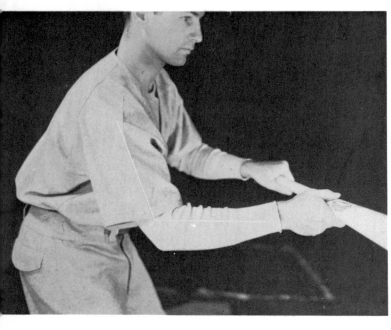

Photo 5

(Photo 5) should be approximately parallel with the ground, the angle between the forearm and upper arm approximately a right angle.

The correct bunting position for a sacrifice bunt is shown in Photo 6. Your body is slightly crouched, head is up, and eyes on the ball. Your weight is slightly forward, and your arms are relaxed and bent at the elbows, holding the bat parallel to the ground. Now you're ready to bunt.

Photo 6

Photo 7

As the ball approaches, try to keep the bat as level as possible (Photo 7). Get the bat in front of the ball by lowering or raising your body from your knees and waist. Move your arms as little as possible. Let the ball hit the bat. As the ball hits, the bat will recoil into the "V" between the thumb and forefinger of your upper hand (Photo 8). This deadens the impact and prevents the ball from bouncing too far.

Photo 8

Photo 9

In the second type of bunt—the bunt for a base hit—deception is important, so shift your feet as little as possible. After the pitcher has delivered the ball, simply step toward the pitch with your forward foot and bring your bat into bunting position (Photo 9). Now the bunting technique is the same as in the sacrifice bunt. Your lower hand holds firm. Your upper hand holds the bat loosely, and as the ball strikes the bat, the bat recoils back into the upper hand (Photo 10).

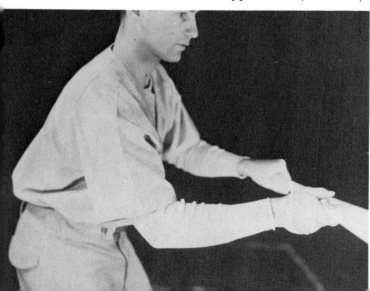

Photo 10

A hitter is the prized member of every team. Whether he is a careful accurate bunter who can put them where he wants them, or the heavy hitter who knocks them out of the park, every batter must know the fundamentals of both hitting and bunting. He must practice them carefully until the patterns of the swing and bunt are natural to him. Then he's a power on any team. Remember, all good hitters have their individual styles, but a consistently good hitter never violates certain basic fundamentals.

The full swing

Photo 1

5. Base Running

There is a one word motto for base runners, and that is "hustle" (Photo 1). When you hit, when the third strike or fourth ball gets by the catcher—hustle! Hustle on everything, and never assume that the throw will beat you. Let the umpire call you out. After you hit, don't measure time in seconds any more—it's split seconds to beat out the throw to first. You can save precious time by getting a good start.

Photo 2

Photo 3

The swing of a right-handed hitter carries him around and away from first base (Photo 2). He can best get his start by pushing off with his left foot and throwing his body in the direction of first base (Photo 3). The left foot starts the drive. The first step comes with the right foot, and from there on it's a straight run down the base line (Photo 4).

Photo 4

Photo 5

A left-handed hitter swings around toward first base and his follow-through sets his momentum in that direction (Photo 5). He can capitalize on that advantage by pushing off on the ball of his right foot and leaning his body in the direction of his run, as shown in Photo 6. He then takes his first step with his left foot (Photo 7).

During the run to first base, if your hit is to the right side of the diamond, you can easily tell what's happening to the ball.

Photo 6

Photo 7

If your hit is to the left side, a quick glance over your shoulder without slackening speed will help you decide what to do at first base (Photo 8). If it looks as though it will be close at first, take a straight line to the bag, just a little to the right of the foul

Photo 8

97

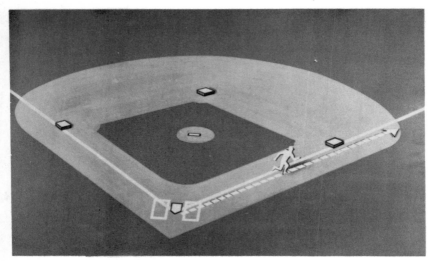

Running to first base only

line, and don't try to stop. Run straight through along the right field line and don't let up speed until you have touched the bag.

As you approach first base, you may see the possibility of advancing to second. As soon as you see this, swing out to the

The arc toward second

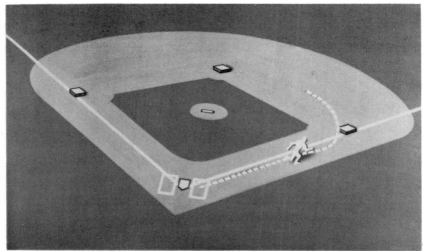

Photo 9

right to start a flat arc that will cut the inside corner of first
base, and continue in an easy curve toward second. Photo 9
shows how you start the arc as you come down the first base
line. Lean your weight slightly to the right and take a couple
of steps at an angle into foul territory.

As you round the bag, try to hit the inside corner with
whichever foot is most convenient in your stride. Don't try to
hit the bag with a certain foot (Photo 10).

Photo 10

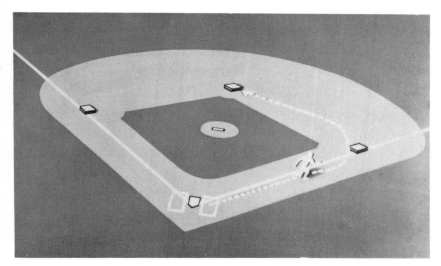

Around the bases in a flat arc

Photo 11

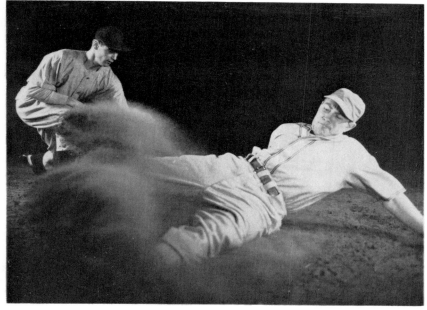

Photo 12

SLIDING

The run from first through second, third and home is merely a continuation of the same flat arc you started at first base. If you have to hustle to beat the throw into second, that arc should straighten out as you take the shortest possible route to the base. If the play is very close at second, you should slide, as shown in Photo 11. Sliding is a skill that you can acquire fairly easily. In learning though, remember there is one fundamental rule. *If you decide to slide—slide. Never change your mind.* It's when you change your mind that trouble starts.

There are three basic slides. Photo 12 shows the straight-in slide.

Approach the bag with your body erect and your eyes on the bag. Take off for the slide with whichever foot is most natural to you. In Step 1 the runner is taking off on his right foot.

Step 1

Immediately after the take-off, bend your take-off leg under you. Raise the other leg well off the ground and extend it toward the bag, throwing the upper part of your body backward (Step 2). Be sure the foot of the bent leg is turned sideways to avoid catching the spikes in the ground. Your bent leg

Step 2

Step 3

takes the shock of your fall, and you slide forward on it until your extended leg makes contact with the nearest side of the bag (Step 3). Step 4 shows a bent-leg slide. Use it to reach the bag, and then get back on your feet immediately—ready to go on to the next base if you get the chance. The bent-leg slide is very similar to the straight-in slide with these differences—the take-off is closer to the bag; the extended leg is bent slightly more at the knee; and the upper part of the body is more erect.

BENT-LEG SLIDE

Step 4

As your outstretched leg touches the bag, throw your weight upward and forward until you are back on your feet. Then simply keep on going (Step 5).

Step 1

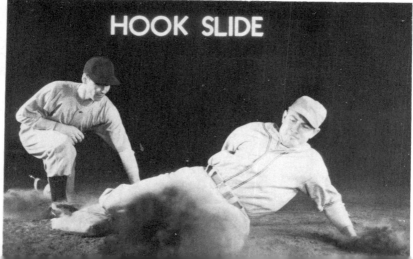

HOOK SLIDE

Step 2

The hook slide, so called because one foot hooks the corner of the bag, is shown in Step 1. It is used to avoid being tagged by a fielder covering a base.

Step 2 shows a player hook sliding to the left. This slider has taken off on his left foot—the foot most natural to him. In the center action both knees are bent; both feet are being turned sideways to avoid catching the spikes in the ground. The upper part of his body is leaning back and his weight is being thrown to the slider's left. The slider hooks the bag with his right foot, thus avoiding the tag (Step 3).

Step 3

Step 4 shows the hook slide to the right. This runner takes off with his left foot—the natural foot for him. In the action on the right, both knees bend under and his feet are turned sideways, throwing his weight to the right. The slider hooks the near corner of the bag with his left foot, avoiding the tag (Step 5).

Step 5

Photo 1

Photo 2

When holding a base, stand with your left foot touching the inside edge of the base and keep it there until the pitcher assumes his pitching position (Photo 1). Then take a lead off the base in a direct line with the next base—as long a lead as you dare take, knowing that you can get back safely if necessary (Photo 2). Stand with your body in good balance, ready to move in either direction quickly. Your feet are spread, and your weight is slightly forward, ready to start for the next base (Photo 3).

Photo 3

Photo 4

Photo 5

To start for the next base, begin by turning the body in the direction of the run (Photo 4). Then push off with your right foot and take your first step with your left foot, driving your body along the base line (Photo 5). Then hustle. Don't let anything stop you from beating out the throw. Make it if it's humanly possible, and don't think it's impossible until you've reached the base (Photo 6). Skill, speed, courage and hustle are what make a good base runner. And good base runners are big factors in winning ball games.

Photo 6

Photo 1

6. Pitching

In defensive play the pitcher is the important man on a ball team, so a pitcher must prepare for his job carefully. Most good pitchers usually use a three-quarter overhand throw. As the ball is released in this throw the throwing arm is in a position between the full overhand position and the sidearm position (Photo 1).

A good pitcher has three basic pitches, and by far the most important of these is his fast ball—just a fast, straight ball, well controlled. Your grip for the fast ball should be the same every time you throw it. Most good pitchers use the one shown in Photo 2. The first two fingers on top grip the ball across the

Photo 2

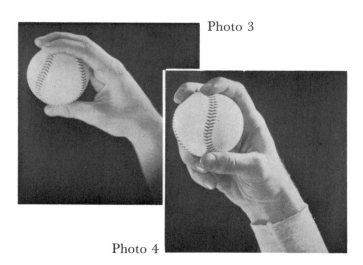

Photo 3

Photo 4

seam at the widest spot. Others grip the ball across the seam at the narrowest spot (Photo 3). The thumb usually contacts another seam directly underneath the fingers (Photo 4).

As your arm comes forward in the pitch, your upper arm is approximately parallel to the ground and the angle between your upper arm and forearm is approximately a right angle. Your body is erect; your eyes on the target (Photo 5). When

Photo 5

Photo 6

you pitch, the ball should leave your hand when it is approximately beside your head, and this is the crucial part of your pitch. This is where you impart the last ounce of energy for speed, and it is your last chance to give the ball direction (Photos 6 and 7). This last movement of the pitch is a snap of the wrist, and it should be practiced first.

Photo 7

To practice the fundamental wrist snap, stand with your upper arm and forearm in that right-angle position and lay your wrist back as far as you can without losing the vertical position of your forearm (Step 1). Then throw the ball, using only your wrist and fingers. Let your hand and fingers feel like the tail end of a cracking whip, and snap the ball as far and as straight as you can (Step 2). Let the ball roll off your fingertips

Step 2

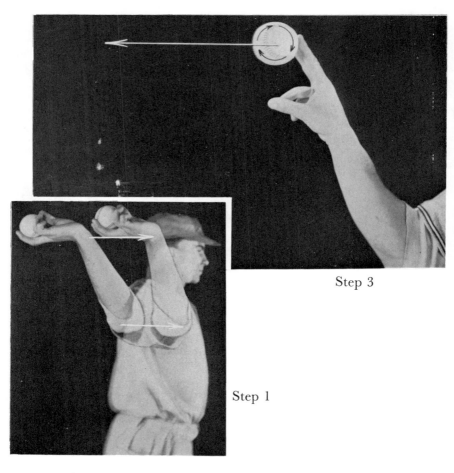

Step 3

Step 1

as you release it, and it will leave your hand with an upward spin (Step 3). The wrist snap for the fast ball is one of the most important fundamentals of pitching.

Now put some arm action into the throw. The arm starts to add power when it comes from a layback position. To practice the arm action, stand with your body comfortably erect and lay your arm back as far as you can with your palm up and your wrist cocked backward. Your elbow leads the forward movement of the throwing arm. Keep your forearm laid back and your wrist cocked, and start your elbow forward (Step 1).

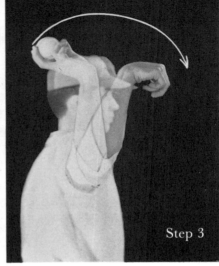

As your elbow comes up even with your shoulder, keep the movement flowing (Step 2).

As your forearm reaches the vertical position, your wrist snaps forward with a decided whipping movement of the hand and fingers (Step 3). Practice the full arm movement, without moving your body, until it feels perfectly natural to you and you can control your pitches (Step 4). Then you're ready for the full pitch.

The pitching movement uses every important muscle in your body, starting in your feet and extending progressively

Step 4

Photo 1

through your legs, hips, shoulders and arm, right out to your fingertips (Photo 1). The timing and coordination of all these muscles in a single, smooth, powerful movement makes the difference between a good pitcher and a mediocre one.

Photo 2 shows the forward stance as you wait for the catcher's signal. Use it when it is not necessary to hold men on bases. In this stance your right foot is on the pitcher's plate with the front spike extended over the front edge. Your left foot is directly behind the plate and all your weight is on your back foot. Keep the ball hidden from the batter (Photo 3).

Photo 2

Photo 3

Step 1   Step 2

The pitch starts with a shift of the weight to the forward foot. As you shift, bend forward at the waist and let the arms swing back naturally. At the same time, bend your knees slightly. You *may* shift your rear foot backward (Step 1). Now reverse the action. Shift your weight back to the rear foot, straighten up at the waist and start your arms swinging in a low full arc that will finish over your head. The gloved hand comes up in front of the ball (Step 2).

Swing your arms upward until your hands are comfortably above your head in what is called the stretch position, still keeping your eyes on the target. During this upward swing your right foot turns outward until, at the stretch position, it is almost at a right angle to the direction of your pitch (Step 3). A slight pause here—and then the pitch.

Step 3   116

In the full pitching movement from the stretch, your body winds back as your arm goes into the layback position. At the same time your body starts forward in a long stride, adding the force of the moving body to the speed of your arm and wrist as you release the ball. Continue your motion with a full follow-through.

The pitching movement starts as you bring your left knee up close across your body and start your throwing arm swinging down and back toward its layback position. At the same time your body pivots around to point your left shoulder at the target (Step 1). As your weight shifts onto your right foot, push

Step 1

117

Step 2

off with that foot, launching your body in the direction of the pitch (Step 2). Now stride forward, directly toward the plate, with your cocked left leg, bringing your throwing arm to the layback position (Step 3). Now your body is moving forward fast.

Step 3

Step 4

As soon as your left foot touches the ground, start uncoiling your body. The weight is now on your left foot. Your hips and shoulders pivot around square with the plate (Step 4). At the same time start your throwing arm whipping through toward the release point. Your elbow is now leading the arm movement (Step 5).

Step 5

Release the ball with a snap of the wrist (Step 6). Thus as the ball is released, everything is moving forward—body, shoulder, arm, hand and right foot —as all the power of your body goes into a controlled pitch (Step 7). But don't stop here, or even slow up. Follow through. Throw the pitching arm forward and down, and the right foot

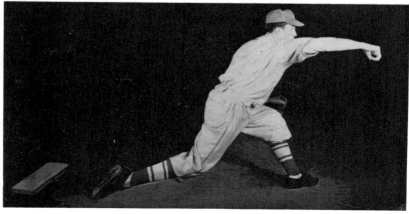

Step 8

will start swinging forward naturally (Step 8). The follow-through ends with your right foot up almost even with your left and your weight well under control, ready to field the ball if it should be hit in your direction (Step 9).

Step 9

In the complete pitching movement the steps are: One—weight forward. Two—weight back for the stretch. Three—knee cocked and everything coiled back. Four—the stride and five—the pitch. Everything smoothly and powerfully uncoils in a whiplike action that starts in the rear foot, travels through your body and arm and ends in the follow-through.

Photo 1

Photo 2   Photo 3

When it's necessary to hold a runner or runners on base, you will have to use a sideward stance and slightly different sequence of movement in your pitch. In the sideward stance your right foot is against the front of the rubber and your left is a comfortable distance ahead. Your weight rests evenly on both feet (Photo 1). From this position you may raise your arms overhead first (Photo 2).

Then drop your hands down into a resting position close to your body, your arms relaxed against the sides of your body, the ball in contact with your throwing hand and your glove (Photo 3). The position of the feet may be in the open stance with the left foot slightly toward first base, as in Photo 3, or in the parallel stance shown in Photo 4. The open stance is commonly used to hold a runner on first base. The closed

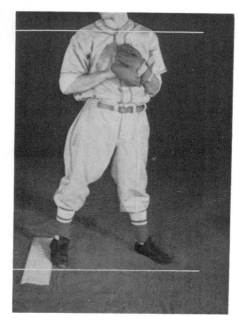

Photo 4

stance is most commonly used to hold a man on second, although many good pitchers use several variations of this principle.

To start the pitch from the sideward stance, don't cock your knee. Simply shift your weight back to the right foot and let your pitching arm swing back into the layback position. From there your stride is straight forward toward the plate—long and

Photo 5

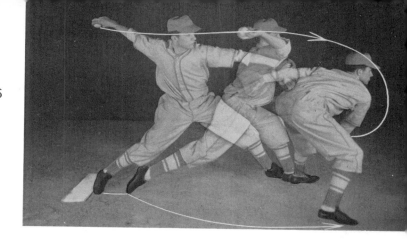

Photo 6

low. The knee-cock is practically eliminated (Photo 5). After the stride (Photo 6) the arm and body movements are exactly the same as in the pitch from the forward stance.

The first requirement of any pitcher is a well controlled fast ball from both the forward and sideward stance. After you have mastered it you can go on to the curve and change of pace.

A curve is a pitch in which you give the ball a spin that makes it change direction as it nears the plate. To throw a curve (Photo 1) you follow the same basic fundamentals that you use in your fast ball with two exceptions—the grip, and the action of hand and wrist on delivery.

CURVE BALL

Photo 1

Photo 2

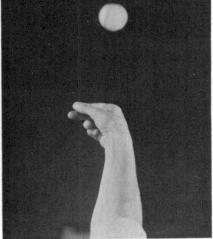

Photo 3

Your grip is similar to the fast ball grip, except that you exert considerably more pressure with the second finger than with the index finger (Photo 2). And as you deliver the ball you twist your hand inward from the wrist at the same time as the wrist snap. The ball rolls off the outside of your first finger, thus developing the spin that makes it change direction on its way to the plate (Photo 3).

The change-of-pace ball is pitched with a delivery that looks like a fast ball but it travels more slowly (Photo 1). Some pitch-

CHANGE OF PACE

Photo 1

Photo 2

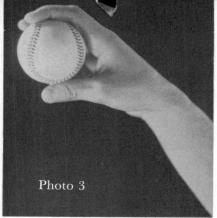

Photo 3

ers grip the ball loosely and well back in the hand for a change-of-pace ball and deliver it with very little pressure by the fingers—somewhat like a shot-put delivery (Photo 2). Others keep the normal grip and achieve the change of pace through the action of their fingers as they release the ball (Photo 3). Just as they release the ball they relax their fingers, thus taking some of the speed off the ball (Photo 4).

The fast ball, the curve and the change-of-pace ball—once mastered with speed and control—provide variety enough for good defensive baseball. Practice them well, study your movements constantly to make sure they contain all the fundamentals, and you are well on your way to successful pitching.

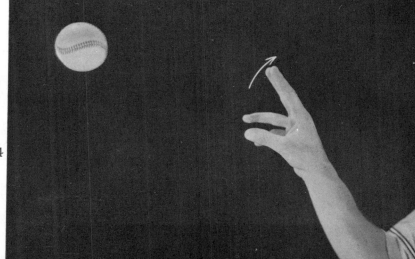

Photo 4

Photo 1

7. Catching

In every baseball game the catcher is the key strategist of defensive play. If you are a catcher, be as close as possible to the batter without interfering with him. In this position you are able to present a better target to the pitcher and, close to the plate, you can handle low pitches and foul tips better (Photo 1).

While giving signals to the pitcher, be in a squat position with your feet comfortably apart, knees turned out, and left forearm resting on your thigh. Your gloved hand extends beyond your left knee. Your throwing hand gives the signal in front of your crotch or alongside either of your legs (Photo 2).

Photo 2

Photo 3

As soon as the signal for the pitch is given, raise up a little from the squat position and take a comfortable stance with your feet well spread apart, your right foot slightly behind the left (Photo 3). Your throwing hand should be relaxed and the fingers closed loosely around your thumb. Don't clench your fist; just let your thumb relax behind your index finger (Photo 4). Don't change the position of your hands until after the pitcher has started his delivery. If the pitch is below the waist, your gloved hand should be held out with the palm toward the pitcher, fingers pointing down. If the pitch is above the waist,

Photo 4

the fingers of your gloved hand should point upward (Photo 5).

Photo 6

Photo 5

To catch the ball, simply roll your right hand around to the front of the glove and trap the ball in the pocket (Photo 6). As the right hand swings over to hold the ball, the fingers automatically encircle the ball in the correct throwing position (Photo 7).

In throwing, use a snap overhand throw whenever possible. It gets the ball away faster. Your fastest throwing action is the same snap overhand throw you learned earlier from the throwing unit of this series.

Photo 7

From the receiving position get your arm, body and feet into the layback position the shortest possible way.

Avoid the full swing if possible. It wastes time and may hurry you to the point where you sacrifice control (Photo 8).

Photo 8

Photo 9

Photo 10

Step 1

From the layback position make a snap overhand throw with all your power (Photo 9).

One of the most important requirements of a good catcher is that he must be able to throw. But throwing presents special problems to a catcher because he usually has a batter in front of him to obstruct his throw (Photo 10). To get around the batter there are certain fundamental movements in a catcher's footwork. The following photographs show some of the more complicated movements.

If you have a right-handed batter at the plate and the pitch is outside—to your right—here is your footwork for a throw. From your catching position you step to the right with the right foot to catch the ball. This takes you clear of the batter (Step 1). From this position take one step forward with the left

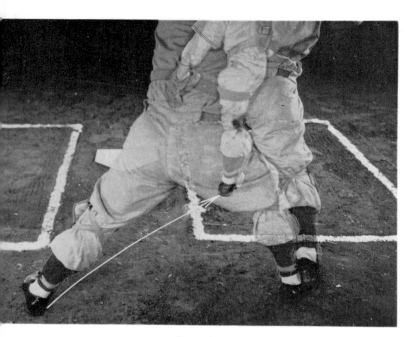

Step 2

*Catching
an inside
pitch*

Low and inside

foot and throw (Step 2). The footwork for a throw to the right, with an outside pitch and a right-handed batter, is then a step to the right with the right foot to catch the ball, and a step forward with the left foot for the throw.

With a right-handed batter and an inside pitch, a different pattern of footwork is required for the throw. First, step to the left to make the catch and then to the right with the right foot, then forward with the left to throw.

If you have a right-handed batter and an inside pitch and you want to throw to third base, the batter is very much in

Step 1

Step 2

136

Step 3

your way. To avoid him, take a step to the left with the left foot
to get into position for the catch (Step 1). Then, with the right
foot step diagonally left and back until your right foot is
behind your left. This takes you clear of the batter (Step 2).
Now step toward third with your left foot and throw behind the
hitter (Step 3).

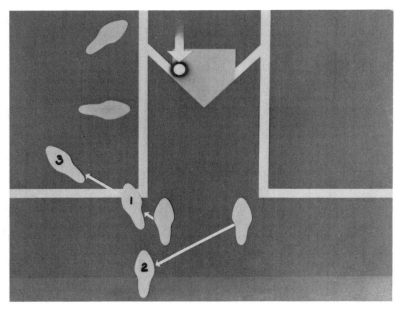

The complete movement for a throw to third with a right-handed batter and an inside pitch. Step left to make the catch, diagonally back and left with the right foot, then toward third with the left foot to make the throw.

With a left-handed batter and an inside pitch, your throw to second base requires a specific footwork pattern to avoid the batter. A step to the right with the right foot puts you in position for the catch (Step 1). From here, shift your weight back to the left foot. Then, in quick succession, step diagonally forward and to the left with your right foot (Step 2) and step forward toward second base with your left for the throw (Step 3). As you become more familiar with this footwork the last two steps will become a jump shift—a 1-2 count instead of a 1-2-3 count.

Step 1

Steps 2 and 3

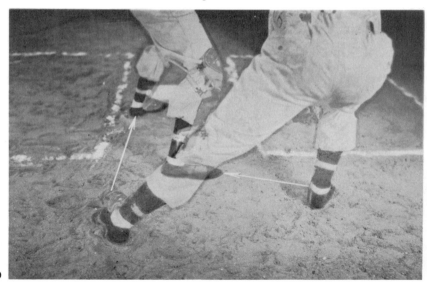

Step 1

Step 2

140

Photo 1

For a throw to second from an outside pitch to a left-handed hitter, step left to catch the ball first (Step 1). Then swing your right foot diagonally back behind the left as you lay back for the throw (Step 2). Now step forward with the left foot and throw.

On a throw to first base, you can step behind the batter, as shown in Photo 1. If the pitch is to the outside the catcher may throw in front of the batter.

Photo 2

As a catcher you will handle many fly balls. The first thing you must do is flip off your mask (Photo 2) and toss it in the direction opposite the ball. Then get under the ball fast and wait for it, remembering the infield drift. A fly ball in the home plate area has a strong spin toward the infield. As the ball comes down, it will break toward the infield. Therefore, adjust your waiting position accordingly.

A catcher waits for a fly ball in front of the plate, playing it over his head.

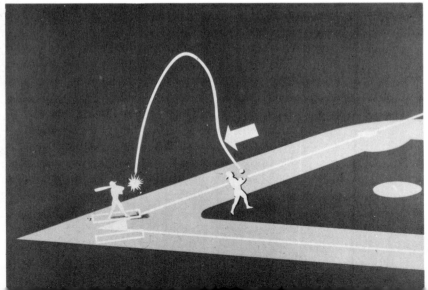

As a catcher you will handle many bunts too. Start immediately for any bunt in your area. If the bunted ball is rolling, place your glove in front of it and scoop it into your mitt with your throwing hand. If it has stopped rolling, pick it up with your throwing hand. Use this method only on a fast play, however, for two hands should be used whenever possible.

Scooping up the ball

In a force play at home plate, that is, if a runner from third base is being forced home and it is not necessary to tag him, stand with your left foot on the front of the plate, facing in the direction of the throw (Step 1). Keep your left foot on the plate

Step 1

and step forward with your right foot as you receive the ball. Then to complete the double play, pivot on your right foot and throw to first base (Step 2).

Step 2

When covering home plate in defensive play, a catcher should know the technique of tagging a runner. To tag a runner coming into the plate, first place yourself in a position facing the throw (Step 1). To tag him, drop low, holding the ball firmly with both hands and the back of your glove toward the incoming runner. Never tag a runner with *one* hand unless it is the only possible way to get him in time (Step 2).

Another very important part of a catcher's job has nothing to do with technique. He is the only player who faces all the others, and he is the defensive strategist in emergencies. So to him falls the job of maintaining much of the team's morale. If you are a catcher, be full of pep and enthusiasm and, at the same time, calm enough to make sound decisions quickly.

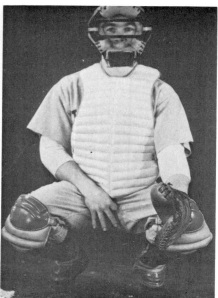

Encouraging the pitcher *Giving his signals*

Catching is a big part of baseball. When learning to be a catcher, learn the fundamental skills of the position thoroughly. Practice them until they are instinctive because, as the team's strategist, you'll have other things to think of during a game.

Excerpts from "Little League Baseball Handbook"

Published by permission of Little League Baseball, Inc.

FEDERAL CHARTER

By virtue of legislation approved unanimously by both the House of Representatives and the Senate and signed into law by President Lyndon B. Johnson on July 16, 1964, Little League Baseball has been granted a Congressional Charter of Federal Incorporation.

AGE BRACKET

Any boy who does not reach his 13th birthday before August 1st of the current year is eligible to try out for Little League. From 13 to 15 years of age, a boy is eligible for the Senior Division.

ELIGIBILITY

The boy must live within the physical boundaries described for the local league and must have parental consent.

REGISTRATION

Each local league will provide an adequate period for the registration of all boys of Little League age in the league's territory. Proper notification of the registration, time and place must be made through normal channels, schools, etc., for such notice.

TRYOUTS

All registered boys must have opportunity to take part in the league's tryouts for eventual selection to teams. Such tryouts are conducted by managing personnel of the league in order to evaluate the playing skills and ability of the player candidates.

PLAYER SELECTION

On the basis of tryouts, comparative point values are placed on each candidate. Managers are then free to compete in an "auction," or some similarly equitable bidding, for players. Selection on this basis continues until such time as the prescribed rosters of each team in the league have been filled.

MINOR LEAGUES

Boys who are not selected for the league teams, or perhaps lack sufficient maturity, skills or other attributes, may be retained in the program for training by means of a "farm" or "minor league" system operated by and in conjunction with the regular Little League program.

THE PLAYERS

Any boy who will attain the age of 9 years before August 1 and who will not attain the age of 13 years before August 1 of the year in question shall be eligible to compete in Little League Baseball. This means that a boy who will be 13 years old on August 1 or later is eligible to play that year; a boy who will be 13 years old on July 31 or earlier, will not be eligible for either local league play or tournament play at any time during the calendar year in question.

Girls are not eligible.

MINOR LEAGUE

Any boy who will attain the age of 8 years before August 1 and who will not attain the age of 13 years before August 1 shall be eligible to compete. A boy whose name appears on a major league roster shall not be permitted to play with a minor league team.

OFFICIAL PLAYING RULES

2.00—THE PLAYING FIELD

A. The distance between all bases shall be sixty (60') feet.

B. The distance between the point of home plate and front side of pitcher's plate shall be forty-six (46') feet.

4.00—DEFINITION OF TERMS

4.02—*Appeal* is the act of a defensive team or player claiming a violation of the rules by an offensive player.

4.05—A *Balk* is an illegal act by the pitcher with a runner or runners on base, entitling all runners to advance one base.

4.22—A *Fair Ball* is a legally batted ball that settles on fair ground between home and first base, or between home and third base, or that is on or over fair territory when bounding to the outfield past first base or third base, or that touches first or third base, or that first falls on fair territory on or beyond first base or third base; or that, while on or over fair territory, touches the person of an umpire or player. A fair fly must be judged according to the relative position of the ball and the foul line, including the foul pole, and not as to whether the fielder is on fair or foul territory at the time he touches the ball.

4.25—A *Fielder's Choice* is the act of a fielder who handles a fair grounder and, instead of throwing to first base to retire the batter-runner, throws to another base in an attempt to retire a preceding runner. The term is also used by scorers (a) to account for the advance of the batter-runner who takes one or more extra bases when the fielder who handles his safe hit attempts to retire a preceding runner; and (b) to account for the advance of a runner (other than by stolen base or error) while a fielder is attempting to retire another runner.

4.27—A *Force Play* is a play in which a runner legally loses his right to occupy a base by reason of the batter's becoming a base runner. (The batter is the only player who can start a force play. First base must be occupied by a base runner or it is not a force play.)

4.28—A *Forfeited Game* is a game declared ended by the Umpire-in-Chief in favor of the offended team by a score of 6–0 for violation of the rules.

4.29—A *Foul Ball* is a legally batted ball that settles on foul territory between home and first base, or between home and third base, or that bounds past first or third base on or over foul territory, or that first falls on foul territory beyond first or third base, or, while on or over foul territory, touches the person of an umpire or a player, or any object foreign to the natural ground. A foul fly shall be judged according to the relative position of the ball and the foul line, including the foul pole, and not as to whether the fielder is on foul or fair territory at the time he touches the ball.

4.31—A *Foul Tip* is a ball batted by the batter that goes sharp and direct from the bat to the catcher's hands and is legally caught. It is not a foul tip unless caught. A foul tip is a strike and the ball is alive. If not caught, it is a foul and the ball is dead. It is not a catch if it is a rebound from any part of the catcher's equipment other than the catcher's glove or hand. This rule shall be followed to the letter, and it shall not be interpreted to allow a smothered catch to count as a catch.

4.35—An *Illegal Pitch* is:

1. A pitch delivered to the batter when the pitcher does not have his pivot foot in contact with the pitcher's plate.

2. When the pitcher delivers the pitch with a foreign substance applied to the ball. Rosin can be applied to the hand.

3. A quick return pitch.

4. An interrupted motion.

Note: If batter reaches base safely and other runners advance at least one base, the pitch becomes legal.

4.36—An *Illegally Batted Ball* is one hit by the batter with one or both feet on the ground entirely outside the lines of the batter's box.

4.38—An *Infield Fly* is an out called by the umpire on the batter if, before two are out, while first and second or first, second and third bases are occupied, he hit a fair fly ball, other than a line drive, that in the judgment of the umpire can reasonably be caught by an infielder. Where a defensive player who normally plays in the outfield places himself in the infield, he shall for the purpose of the Infield-Fly rule be considered an infielder. In such case the umpire shall declare it an *Infield Fly*. However, the runners may be off their bases or advance at the risk of the ball being caught, the same as on any other fly ball. If a runner is hit by the ball while standing on base, he shall not be called out, but the ball is dead and the batter shall be called out; but if a base runner is hit while off base, both he and the batter shall be called out and the ball is dead. Provided that with first and second bases occupied, or first, second and third bases occupied, before two are out, any attempt to bunt which results as a fair fly ball shall not be regarded as an Infield-Fly.

4.41—In *Jeopardy* is a term indicating that the ball is in play and an offensive player may be put out.

4.45—*Obstruction* is the illegal act of a fielder who, while not in possession of the ball and not in the act of fielding the ball, impedes the progress of any runner.

4.56—The *Pitcher's Pivot Foot* is that foot which is in contact with the pitcher's plate or rubber as he delivers the pitch to the batter.

4.58—A *Quick Return Pitch* is a pitch made with obvious intent to catch a batter off balance. It is an illegal pitch.

4.62—A *Run-Down* is the act of the defense in attempting to put out an offensive player between bases.

4.65—A *Strike* is a legal pitch which meets any of these conditions:

A. It is struck at by the batter and is missed.

B. It enters the strike zone in flight and is not struck at.

C. It is fouled by the batter when he has less than two strikes.

D. It is bunted foul. (The batter is out and the ball is dead, if he bunts foul on the third strike.)

E. It hits the batter's person as he strikes at it. (Dead ball.)

    1. Touches the batter in flight in the strike zone.

    2. Becomes a foul tip.

F. It becomes a foul tip.

4.74—*Little League Pitching Position.* The Little League pitcher shall assume a position facing the batter with his pivot foot on or in front of and in contact with, but not off the end of the pitcher's plate. From this position any natural movement associated with delivery of the ball to the batter commits him to the pitch. He shall not raise either foot from the ground, except that in his actual delivery of the ball to the batter he may take one step backward, and one step forward with his free foot.

6.00—THE GAME—GENERAL

6.02—All defensive players, except the catcher, must be in fair territory when the ball is put in play.

A. The catcher must stand within the catcher's box until the ball leaves the pitcher's hand.

B. The pitcher must be in legal position while in the act of delivery.

C. When the ball is in play, no offensive player shall cross the catcher's line except the batter or a runner who is trying to score.

6.03—After an umpire calls "Play," the ball is alive and in play and remains so until an umpire calls "Time" for a legal cause. Then the ball is dead, there can be no play—no player may be put out, no bases run or runs scored, except that runners may advance or return as legally provided.

6.13—It is a *Regulation Game* when:

A. The home team shall have scored more runs in five innings than the visiting team has scored in six innings.

B. The home team scores the winning run in the sixth inning before the inning is completed. If a batter in the last half of the final inning of a game hits a home run over the fence or into a stand, all runners on base at the time, as well as the batter, shall be entitled to score, but to score legally, all bases must be touched in order by all runners. The final score of such game shall be the total number of runs made by each team.

C. If the score is tied at the end of six completed innings, play is continued until one team has scored more runs than the other in an equal number of innings; provided, that if the home team scores the winning run before the third man is out in any inning after the sixth, the game shall terminate and be a regulation game.

D. Terminated by the umpire on account of weather, darkness, or any other cause which makes further play impossible, provided four or more innings have been played, or the home team has scored more runs in three innings, or before the completion of its fourth inning, than the visiting club has scored in four completed innings.

E. The umpire terminates play after four completed innings. The score of such game shall be the score at the end of the last completed inning. If, however, the home team shall have scored more total runs than the visiting team when the game is terminated while the home team is at bat, the score of such game shall be the total runs scored by each team. Also, when a game is terminated after five completed innings, with the visiting team at bat and the home team ahead, the score shall be the total number of runs scored by each team at the time the game is terminated.

6.15—The Umpire-in-Chief shall declare a game forfeited in favor of the opposing team once play has begun, when a team:

A. Refuses to continue to play.

B. Fails to, or is unable to, continuously field nine eligible players.

C. Uses methods to delay or shorten the game.

D. After being warned by the umpire, wilfully continues to violate rules.

7.00—THE GAME—OFFENSE

7.02—One run shall score every time a runner, after having legally touched the first three bases, shall legally touch home plate before three are out. A run does not count under any of these conditions:

A. If the runner reaches home plate on or during a play in which the third man is put out on a force.

B. If the batter fails to reach first base safely and makes a third out.

C. If a preceding runner makes a third out by failing to touch a base (appeal play).

7.05—The Batting Order must be followed throughout the game unless a player is substituted for another. Substitutes must take the place of the replaced player in the batting order.

7.06—A player whose name is on his team's Batting Order may not become a substitute runner. The so-called "courtesy runner" is not permitted.

7.07—The first batter in each inning after the first inning shall be the player whose name follows that of the last player in the batting order to legally complete his time at bat in the previous inning.

> *Note:* In the event that a third out is made by a base runner while a batter is in the batter's box, regardless of the count on the batter, he shall be the first batter of the next inning and the count of balls and strikes shall start over.

7.09—A batter is out when:

A. His fair or foul fly ball (other than foul tip) is legally caught by any player of the opposing team.

B. He bats the ball illegally. Dead ball, runners may not advance. There is no penalty and the ball is not dead, if the batter does not actually hit the ball—either fair or foul. An illegally batted ball is one hit by the batter with one or both feet on the ground entirely outside of the batter's box.

C. He has three strikes, either called or swinging. The catcher does not have to catch the third strike. The batter is out, but the ball is in play and runners may advance at their own risk.

D. He bunts foul on the third strike.

E. He hits an Infield Fly. (See Rule 4.38.)

F. He attempts to hit or bunt a third strike and the ball touches him. The ball is dead, runners cannot advance.

151

G. After hitting or bunting a fair ball, he hits the ball a second time or strikes it with a thrown bat or deflects its course in any way while running to first base. The ball is dead and runners cannot advance. There is no penalty, if interference is not intentional.

H. After a fair hit, he is tagged by a defensive player before he touches first base or first base is tagged by a defensive player who is holding the ball firmly in his hand or glove, before the runner touches the base.

I. A fielder intentionally drops a fly ball or line drive provided there are less than two out and first base is occupied, whether or not other bases are occupied. The force is removed, but runners may advance at their own risk. The runners do not have to tag up.

J. In running the last half of the distance from home base to first base while the ball is being fielded to first base, he runs outside (to the right of) the three-foot line, or inside (to the left of) the foul line, and in the umpire's judgment in so doing interferes with the fielder taking the throw at first base. The ball is dead and runners must return. He may, however, run outside the three-foot line or inside the foul line to avoid a fielder attempting to field a batted ball.

K. He fails to take his position in the batter's box promptly and the following action has taken place. After persistent delay, the umpire shall direct the pitcher to deliver the ball to the batter and every such pitch shall be called "strike" by the umpire, whether or not it enters the strike zone. If the batter enters the batter's box in the interval between any such pitches, the ball and strike count shall continue regularly, but if he has not entered the batter's box when three strikes are called, he shall be declared out.

L. He attempts to hinder the catcher from fielding or throwing the ball by stepping outside the batter's box, or otherwise interferes with that player. The ball is dead and runners cannot advance.

However, he shall not be called out, if despite his interference, the catcher's throw results in a putout, or if the catcher's play results in a putout at home base.

M. He steps from one batter's box to the other while the pitcher is in legal position to pitch.

N. He fails to take his position at bat in the turn in which his name appears on the batting order provided the defensive team appeals to the umpire after the improper batter has completed his turn at bat, but before the first pitch is made to the following batter. If the error is discovered before the improper batter has completed his turn at bat, the proper batter shall replace the man at bat and must assume the count of balls and strikes on the improper batter and no automatic out results.

If, after the improper batter has completed his turn at bat, but before one pitch has been made to the next batter, the defensive team appeals, the proper batter who failed to bat is declared out and the next batter is the man whose name on the batting order follows that of the batter declared out.

7.10—The batter becomes a base runner and is entitled to first base without danger of being put out provided he touches first base when:

A. Four balls have been called by the umpire. This is known as a Base on Balls.

B. The catcher interferes with him, unless he reaches first base safely on a fair hit, an error, or otherwise and no other runner is put out on the play.

If the catcher interferes with the batter by tipping his bat or in any other way, and in spite of this interference, batter reaches first base safely and all other runners are safe also, then disregard the interference.

If the catcher interferes with the batter and either the batter does not reach first safely or any other runner is put out on the play, interference is called. The ball is dead and the batter is given first base and all base runners who are forced to advance are safe. Other runners cannot advance.

Interference is called and the runner is allowed first base, even if he swings and misses, foul tips ball, or hits a foul ball.

C. He is struck by a pitched ball which he is not trying to hit while he is in the batter's box in legal position to bat, provided he makes an honest attempt to avoid being hit by the ball.

If he makes no attempt to avoid being hit by the ball, the umpire shall call the pitch "ball" or "strike" as the case may be.

In either case, the ball is dead and runners may not advance.

D. A fair ball touches an umpire or a runner on fair ground before touching a fielder, provided that if a fair ball touches the umpire after having passed a fielder other than the pitcher, or having touched a fielder (including the pitcher), the ball shall be considered in play. Also, if a fair ball touches the umpire on foul ground, the ball shall be in play.

7.15—When a pitcher is in contact with the pitcher's rubber with the ball in his possession and the catcher in the catcher's box ready to receive delivery of the ball, base runners shall not leave their bases until the ball has been delivered and has reached the batter.

The violation by one base runner shall affect all other base runners.

A. When a base runner leaves his base before the pitched ball has reached the batter and the batter does not hit the ball, the runner is permitted to continue. If a play is made on him and he is out, the out stands. If he reaches the next base safely, he must be returned to the base he occupied before the pitch was made, and no out results.

B. When a base runner leaves his base before the pitched ball has reached the batter and the batter hits the ball the base runner or runners are permitted to continue. If a play is made and the runner or runners are put out, the out or outs will stand. If not put out, the runner or runners must return to the original base or bases or to the unoccupied base nearest the one that was left.

In no event shall the batter advance beyond first base on a single or error, second base on a double or third base on a triple. The Umpire-in-Chief shall determine the base value of the hit ball.

C. When any base runner leaves his base before the pitched ball has reached the batter and the batter bunts or hits a ball within the infield no run shall be allowed to score. If three runners were on the bases and the batter reaches first base safely, each runner shall advance to the base beyond the one he occupied at the start of the play except the runner who occupied third base, which runner shall be removed from the base without a run being scored.

7.16—Each runner except the batter may, without danger of being put out, advance one base when:

A. There is a Balk. (See Rule 8.10.)

B. The batter is allowed first base without danger of being put out and forces the runner to vacate his base. The ball is dead except in the case of a base on balls.

C. The batter hits a fair ball that touches another runner or the umpire before such ball has been touched by or has passed a fielder, if the runner is forced to advance. However, runner hit by batted ball is out.

D. He is obstructed by a fielder, including the catcher. While the ball is dead in respect to this particular runner, it is in play with respect to all other runners.

E. A ball which is thrown by the pitcher while on the pitcher's plate to a base to catch a runner, goes into a stand, a player's bench or over or through a fence or backstop or is touched by a spectator. The ball is dead.

7.17—Each runner including the batter-runner may, without danger of being put out, advance:

A. To home base, if the batter hits a fair fly ball that passes over a fence or into the stands at a distance of 165 feet or more from home base, provided all runners, including the batter, touch all of the bases legally. Or, if a fair fly ball, which in the umpire's judgment would have cleared such fence in flight, is deflected by a defense player who throws his cap, glove or any other article of his apparel the batter shall be awarded a home run.

> *Note:* We recommend that the home run fence be placed at a distance
> of 180 feet at the foul lines and 190 feet at center field. However,
> since this is not always possible, the official distance for home
> runs shall be a minimum of 165 feet.

B. Three bases, if a batted fair ball is touched by a fielder using his cap, glove or any part of his uniform while such article is not in its proper place on his person. However, once the batter has reached third base, the ball is in play, and he may advance to home base at his own risk.

If a fair fly ball, which in the umpire's judgment, would have cleared a fence less than 165 feet from home base in flight, is deflected by a defensive player who throws his cap, glove or any other article of his apparel, all runners shall advance three bases and the ball is dead.

C. Two bases, if the batter hits a fair fly ball that passes over a fence or into the stands at a distance of less than 165 feet from home base. The ball is dead.

D. Two bases, if a fair ball touches a spectator, or if it bounces into the stands outside the first or third base foul lines, or if it goes through or under the fence, the scoreboard, shrubbery or vines on the fence.

E. Two bases, if a live thrown ball is touched by a fielder's use of his cap, glove or any part of his uniform while such article is detached from its proper place on his person. The ball is in play with respect to each runner when he has advanced the two bases allowed. He may advance further at his own risk.

F. Two bases, if a live thrown ball goes into the stands, or into a players' bench, or over or through a fence (whether the ball rebounds into the field or not), or remains in the meshes of a wire screen protecting the spectators. The ball is dead.

G. One base, if a ball which is pitched to the batter goes into a stand, a players' bench or over or through a fence or backstop, or is touched by a spectator. The ball is dead. If such a wild pitch is ball four, the batter-runner is entitled to first base only.

7.20—Any base runner is out when:

A. He runs more than three feet away from a direct line between bases to avoid being tagged, unless his action is to avoid interference with a fielder fielding a batted ball.

B. He intentionally interferes with a thrown ball, or hinders a fielder attempting to make a play on a batted ball. The ball is dead and other runners must return.

In addition, if in the umpire's judgment, the attempted play would have resulted in a putout had the runner not interfered, the runner on whom the play was being made shall also be declared out.

C. He is tagged with a live ball while off his base. The ball must be securely held by the fielder before and after the tag. If the impact of the runner breaks the base loose from its legal position, "no play can be made on that runner if he had reached that base safely."

> *Note:* The runner is safe if he has reached the base before his impact
> breaks the base loose and breaking the base loose would be the
> cause of his being put out.

D. He fails to retouch his base after a fair or foul ball is legally caught on the fly, before he or his base is tagged by defensive player. An appeal play.

E. He fails to reach the next base before a defensive player tags him or the base, if he is forced to advance by reason of the batter becoming a base runner. However, if there is no force, or if the force is removed by reason of a following runner or runners having been put out, the base runner must be tagged to be put out.

F. He is touched by a fair batted ball before it is touched by the pitcher, or before it has touched or passed an infielder, even if he is on his base. The ball is dead and no run may score nor runners advance except runners who are forced to advance by the batter becoming a base runner.

G. He is hit by a declared Infield-Fly while off his base. Both the runner and the batter are out. He is not out, if he is on his base when hit by a declared Infield-Fly, but the batter is out.

H. He attempts to score on play in which the batter interferes with the play at home plate with less than two out. When two are out, the batter is out unless the catcher, despite the interference puts out the base runner attempting to score. If the catcher is unable to put out the runner attempting to score, the interference puts the batter out and the run does not count.

I. He passes a preceding runner before such runner is out.

J. After he has acquired legal possession of a base, he must be declared out immediately if he runs the bases in reverse order for the purpose of confusing the defense or making a travesty of the game. The ball is dead and no runner may advance.

K. In running or sliding for home base, he fails to touch home base and makes no attempt to return to the base, provided the defense makes an appeal play.

7.21—On any interference the ball is dead. It is interference by a batter or runner and the batter or runner is out when:

A. After a third strike he hinders the catcher in his attempt to field the ball.

B. After hitting or bunting a ball fair; his bat hits the ball a second time in fair territory. The ball is dead and no runners may advance. If the batter-runner drops his bat and the ball rolls against the bat in fair territory and, in the umpire's judgment, there was no intent to interfere with the course of the ball, the ball is alive and in play.

After batting or bunting a ball foul, in the judgment of the umpire, he intentionally deflects the course of the ball in any manner while running to first base, the ball is dead and no runner may advance.

C. Before two are out and a runner on third base, the batter hinders a fielder in making a play at home base, the runner is out.

D. Any member or members of an offensive team stand or otherwise collect around any base to which a runner is advancing, to confuse, interfere or add to the difficulty of the defensive player.

E. In the judgment of the umpire, the coachers at first or third base, by touching or holding the runner, physically assists him in returning to, or leaving, third base or first base. The runner, however, shall not be declared out if no play is being made on him.

F. With a runner on third base, the coacher leaves his box and acts in any manner to draw a throw by a defensive player.

G. In running the last half of the distance from home base to first base while the ball is being fielded to first base he runs outside (to the right of) the three foot line, or inside (to the left of) the foul line and, in the umpire's judgment, interferes with the fielder taking the throw at first base, or attempting to field a batted ball.

H. He fails to avoid a fielder who is attempting to field a batted ball, or intentionally interferes with a thrown ball; provided, that if two or more fielders attempt to field a batted ball, and the runner comes in contact with one or more of them, the umpire shall determine which fielder is entitled to the benefit of this rule, and shall not declare the base runner out for coming in contact with a fielder other than the one the umpire determines to be entitled to field such a ball.

I. A fair hit ball touches him before touching a fielder. If a fair ball goes through, or by an infielder, and hits a runner immediately back of him, or hits the runner after having been deflected by a fielder, the umpire must not declare the runner out for being hit by a batted ball. In making such decision the umpire must be convinced that the ball passed through or by the infielder, and that no other infielder had the chance to make a play on the ball. If, in the judgment of the umpire, the runner deliberately and intentionally kicks such a ball on which the infielder has missed a play, then the runner must be called out for interference.

7.22—If players or coaches of an offensive team interfere with a defensive player who is attempting to field a batted or thrown ball or interfere with a thrown ball, "interference" shall be called. The ball is dead. The offensive player on whom the play was being made shall be declared out and other runners may not advance.

7.23—If the umpire behind home plate interferes with the catcher's attempt to throw, the ball is dead and all runners must return.

7.24—Any base runner is out on appeal before the next legal pitch when:
A. After a batted fly ball is caught, he fails to re-touch his base before he or his base is tagged.
B. With the ball in play, while advancing or returning to a base, he fails to touch each base in order before he or a missed base is tagged.
1. No runner may return to touch a missed base after a following runner has scored.
2. When the ball is dead no runner may return to touch a missed base after he has advanced to and touched a base beyond the missed base.
C. He overruns or overslides first base and fails to return to the base immediately, and he or the base, if he attempts to leave the field is tagged.
D. With bases full, batter is awarded base on balls forcing each runner to advance, and runner fails to touch any base to which he is advancing.

> *Note:* An appeal of such out, with less than two outs, must be made before the next pitch occurs. If there are two outs, appeal must be made before all infielders and pitcher have left fair territory.

If appeal causes the third out, then no run shall be allowed to score.

7.25—If a thrown ball accidentally strikes a coacher, the ball is alive.

7.26—If a pitched or thrown ball strikes an umpire, the ball is alive.

7.27—If a pitch is hit foul and is not caught on the fly, the ball is dead and runners must return.

8.00—DEFENSIVE RULES

8.02—A defensive player, other than the pitcher and the catcher, may occupy any position on the playing field in fair territory.

8.03—When a pitcher takes his position at the beginning of a game or when he relieves another pitcher, he shall be permitted up to ten preparatory pitches to his catcher if he so desires. Following this initial warmup, he shall be permitted five pitches between each succeeding inning he works, play to be suspended during all preparatory pitches.

8.04—If a pitcher is replaced, his substitute shall pitch to the batter then at bat until such batter completes his turn at bat or until the inning ends, unless the substitute pitcher is injured and in the judgment of the Umpire-in-Chief cannot continue.

8.05—If the pitcher makes an illegal pitch with the bases unoccupied it shall be called a ball, unless the batter hits the ball and reaches first base safely. The pitch then becomes legal.

8.06—The pitcher shall be removed from the game and grounds if he:

A. Applies a foreign substance of any kind to the ball after warning. However, he may apply rosin to his ungloved hand.

B. Expectorates on the ball, his hand or glove, or wets his fingers with saliva, after warning.

C. Rubs the ball on his glove, person or clothing, after warning.

D. Defaces the ball in any manner.

E. Pitches a "shine" ball, "spit" ball, "mud" ball, or "emery" ball.

F. Persists in intentionally delaying the game by throwing the ball to players other than the catcher when the batter is in position, except in an attempt to retire a base runner, after warning.

G. Pitches at a batter's head or body intentionally.

8.07—The pitcher shall not pitch the "Quick Return Ball." If he tries it, he shall be warned once by the umpire, without penalty. If repeated, each such pitch shall be called "ball" unless the batter reaches first on a fair hit, an error or otherwise.

8.08—The pitcher shall not be permitted to wear a shirt with ragged, frayed or split sleeves. He shall not attach tape or any other material of a color different from his uniform or glove, to his glove or clothing.

8.09—If, with the bases unoccupied, the pitcher delays the game by failing to deliver the ball to the batter within 20 seconds after assuming pitching position, the umpire shall call "Ball."

8.10—A balk shall be called if, with one or more runners, the pitcher:

A. While touching his plate, makes any motion naturally associated with his pitch and fails to deliver the ball.

B. While touching his plate, feints a throw to *First* base and fails to complete the throw.

C. While touching his plate, fails to step directly toward any base before throwing to that base.

D. While touching his plate, throws or feints a throw to an unoccupied base, except to make a play.

E. Delivers the ball while his pivot foot is not in contact with the pitcher's plate. The pivot foot must stay in contact with the pitcher's plate from the start of the windup to the delivery of the pitch.

F. Delivers the ball while he is not facing the batter.

G. Makes any motion naturally associated with his pitch while he is not touching the pitcher's plate.

H. Unnecessarily delays the game.

I. Without the ball in his possession stands on or astride the pitcher's plate.

J. Without the ball in his possession, feints a pitch.

K. While touching his plate, accidentally or intentionally drops the ball.

L. Pitches while the catcher is not in his box.

Penalty. When a balk is committed, the ball is dead, and each runner shall advance one base without liability to be put out, unless the batter reaches first base on a hit, an error or otherwise, and all other runners advance at least one base, in which case the play proceeds without reference to the balk.

Index